The Big Lullaby Songbook

Published by
Wise Publications
14-15 Berners Street, London W1T 3LJ,
United Kingdom.

Exclusive Distributors:
Music Sales Limited
Distribution Centre, Newmarket Road,
Bury St Edmunds, Suffolk IP33 3YB,
United Kingdom.
Music Sales Corporation
257 Park Avenue South, New York, NY 10010,
United States of America.
Music Sales Pty Limited
20 Resolution Drive, Caringbah, NSW 2229,
Australia.

Order No. AM993850
ISBN 978-1-84772-581-3
This book © Copyright 2008 Wise Publications,
a division of Music Sales Limited.

Edited by Ann Barkway.
Music processed by Paul Ewers Music Design.
Designed and art directed by Michael Bell Design.
Illustrated by Sonia Canals.
Printed in China.
CD recorded, mixed and mastered by Jonas Persson.
Backing tracks by John Maul.
Vocals by Rachael Parsons.

Your Guarantee of Quality.
As publishers, we strive to produce every
book to the highest commercial standards.
This book has been carefully designed to
minimise awkward page turns and to make playing
from it a real pleasure.
Throughout, the printing and binding have been
planned to ensure a sturdy, attractive publication
which should give years of enjoyment.
If your copy fails to meet our high standards,
please inform us and we will gladly replace it.

www.musicsales.com

"Lay thee down now and rest.
May thy slumbers be blest."

Johannes Brahms

The Big Lullaby
Songbook

Wise Publications
part of The Music Sales Group
London / New York / Paris / Sydney / Copenhagen / Madrid / Tokyo / Berlin

Poems...

Songs...

Teddy Bear, Teddy Bear

Traditional

Ted-dy Bear, ted-dy Bear, turn a-round,___
Ted-dy Bear, Ted-dy Bear, touch the ground.___ Ted-dy Bear, Ted-dy Bear,
show your shoe,___ Ted-dy Bear, Ted-dy Bear, I love you.

Teddy Bear, Teddy Bear, climb the stairs,
Teddy Bear, Teddy Bear, say your prayers.
Teddy Bear, Teddy Bear, turn off the light,
Teddy Bear, Teddy Bear, say goodnight.

Rockabye, Baby

Traditional

9

Lambs Are Sleeping

Traditional

Lul - la - by, oh, lul - la - by,_____

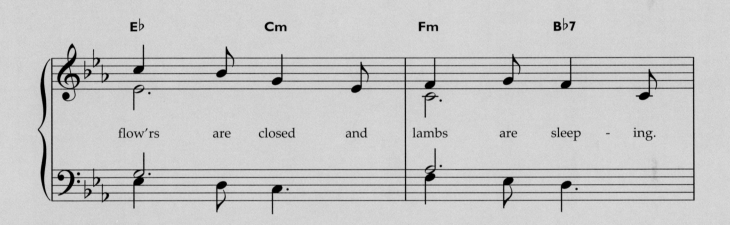

flow'rs are closed and lambs are sleep - ing.

Stars are up, the moon is peep - ing,

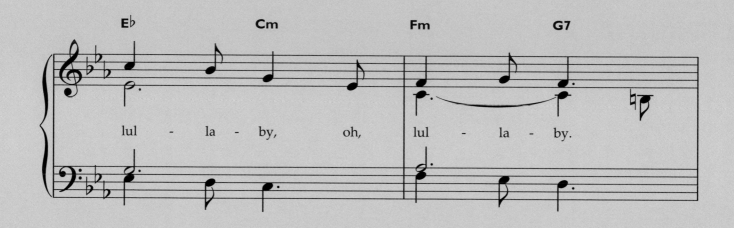

lul - la - by,   oh,   lul - la - by.

While   the   birds   are   si - lence   keep - ing,

sleep,   my   ba - by   fall   a - sleep - ing.

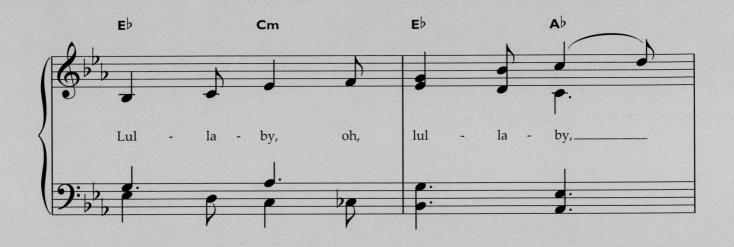

Lul - la - by, oh, lul - la - by,_____

lul - la - by, oh, lul - la - by.

Dance To Your Daddy

Traditional

Chorus

Dance to your dad - dy,

my lit - tle lad - die, dance to your dad - dy, my lit - tle man.

Verse

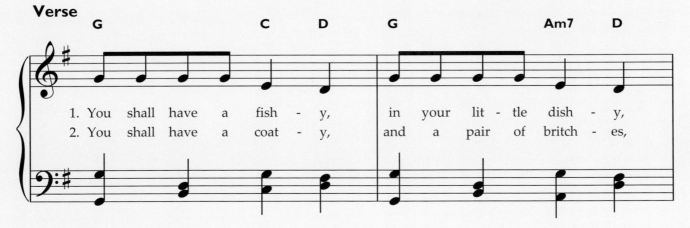

1. You shall have a fish - y, in your lit - tle dish - y,
2. You shall have a coat - y, and a pair of britch - es,

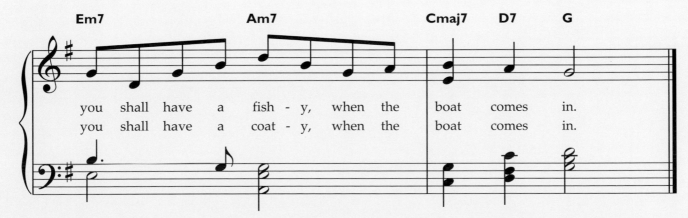

you shall have a fish - y, when the boat comes in.
you shall have a coat - y, when the boat comes in.

15

When you are a man and come to take a wife,
You shall wed a lass and love her all your life.

Hey Diddle Diddle

Traditional

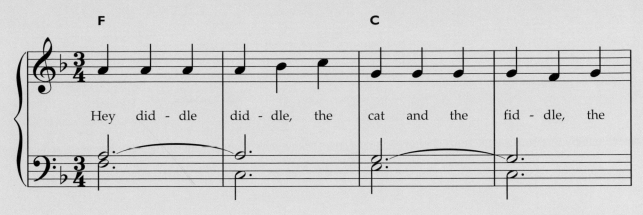

Hey did - dle did - dle, the cat and the fid - dle, the

cow jumped ov - er the moon, _____ The

lit - tle dog laughed__ to see such fun, and the

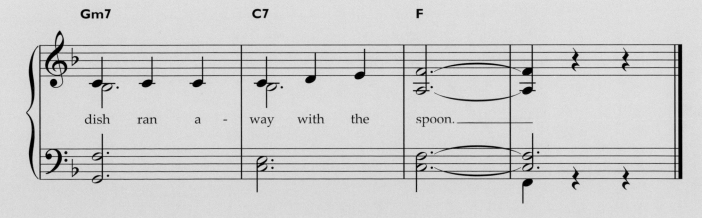

dish ran a - way with the spoon. _____

17

Brahms's Lullaby

Composed by Johannes Brahms

19

All Through The Night

Traditional

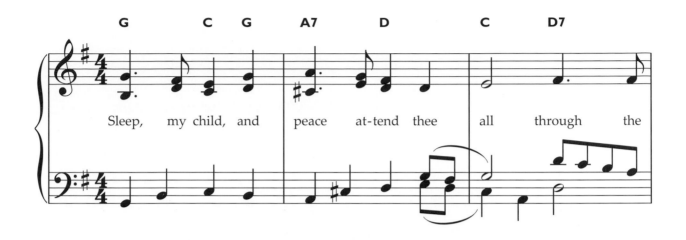

Sleep, my child, and peace at-tend thee all through the

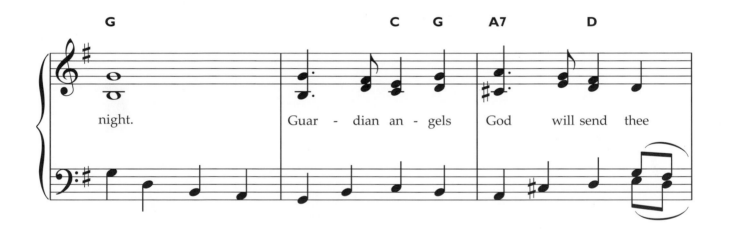

night. Guar - dian an - gels God will send thee

all through the night. Soft and drow - sy

21

hours are creep - ing,   hill and dale in   slum - ber sleep - ing.

I   my lov - ing   vi - gil keep - ing   all   through   the   night.

Angels watching ever round thee, all through the night;

In thy slumbers close surround thee, all through the night.

They should of all fears disarm thee, no forebodings should alarm thee,

They will let no peril harm thee, all through the night.

While the moon her watch is keeping, all through the night,

While the weary world is sleeping, all through the night.

O'er thy spirit gently stealing, visions of delight revealing,

Breathes a pure and holy feeling, all through the night.

22

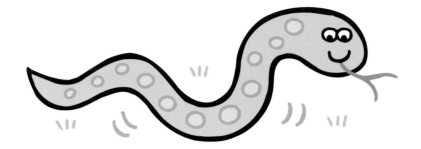

You spotted snakes with double tongue,
Thorny hedgehogs, be not seen;
Newts and blind-worms, do no wrong;
Come not near our fairy queen.

Philomel, with melody,
Sing in our sweet lullaby;
Lulla, lulla, lullaby; lulla, lulla, lullaby!
Never harm,
Nor spell, nor charm
Come our lovely lady night;
So, goodnight, with lullaby.

Lullaby For Titania
From A Midsummer Night's Dream
William Shakespeare

Weaving spiders, come not here;
Hence, you long-legged spinners, hence!
Beetles black, approach not near;
Worm nor snail, do no offence.

Philomel, with melody,
Sing in our sweet lullaby;
Lulla, lulla, lullaby; lulla, lulla, lullaby!
Never harm,
Nor spell, nor charm,
Come our lovely lady night;
So, good night, with lullaby.

Lie-A-Bed

Lie a-bed,
Sleepy head,
Shut up eyes, bo-peep;
Till day-break
Never wake:
Baby, sleep.

Sleepytime

Traditional

Bye Baby Bunting

Traditional

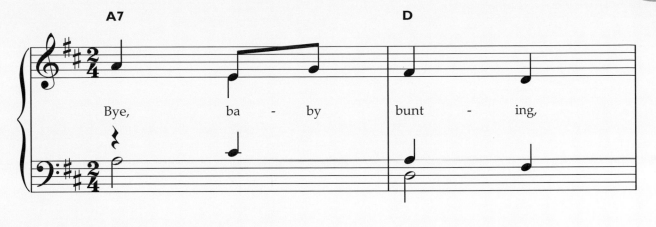

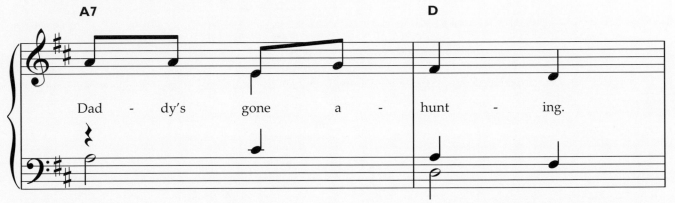

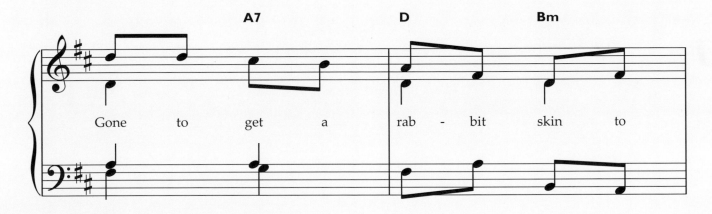

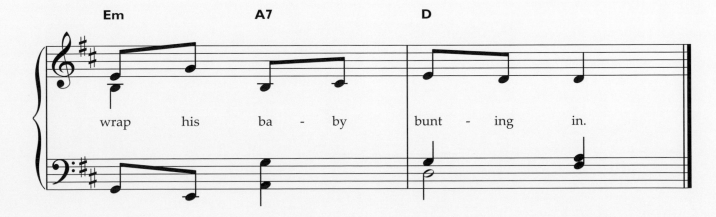

27

Sleep, Little Child

Composed by Wolfgang Amadeus Mozart

29

Rest   on   thy   pil - low   thy   head.

The   world   is   si - lent   and   still;

The   moon   shines bright   on   the   hill,

30

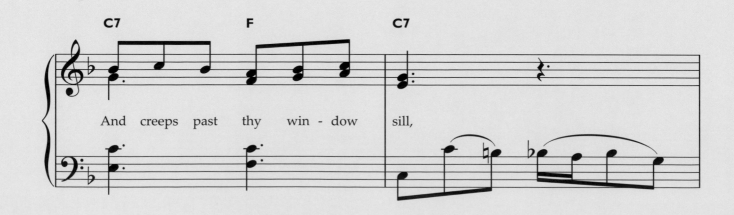

And   creeps past   thy   win - dow   sill,

Sleep, lit - tle child, go to sleep, Oh,

rit.

sleep, go to sleep.

Go Away, Little Fairies

Traditional

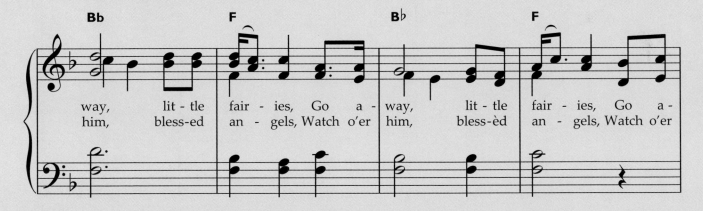

33

Golden Slumbers

Traditional

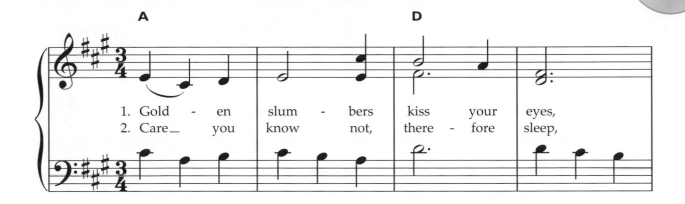

1. Gold - en slum - bers kiss your eyes,
2. Care_ you know not, there - fore, sleep,

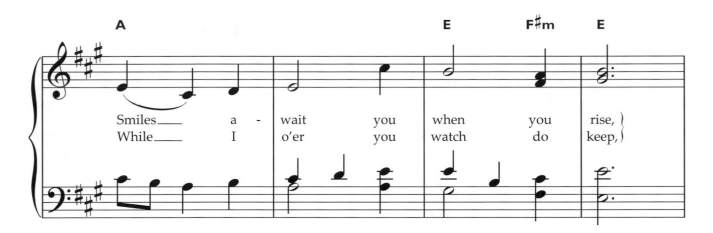

Smiles_ a - wait you when you rise,
While_ I o'er you watch do keep,

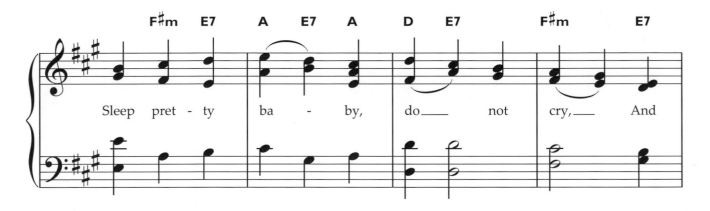

Sleep pret - ty ba - by, do_ not cry,_ And

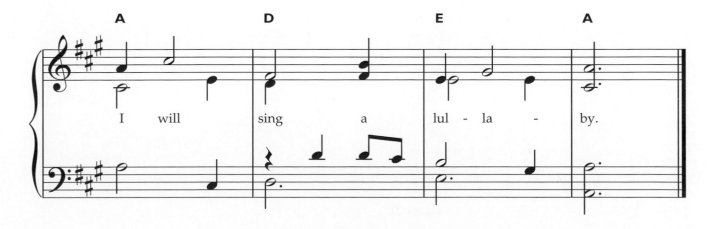

I will sing a lul - la - by.

35

All The Pretty Little Horses

Traditional

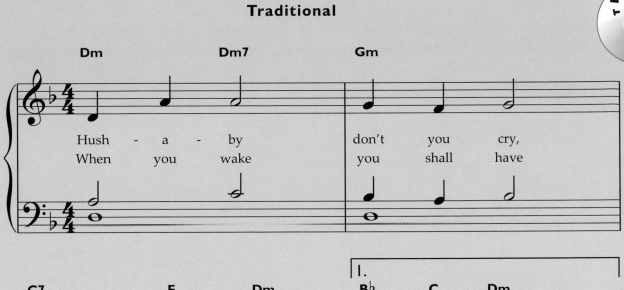

37

Bedtime

Traditional

1. The even-ing is com-ing, The sun sinks to rest, The
2. The flo-wers are clos-ing, The dai-sy's a-sleep, The

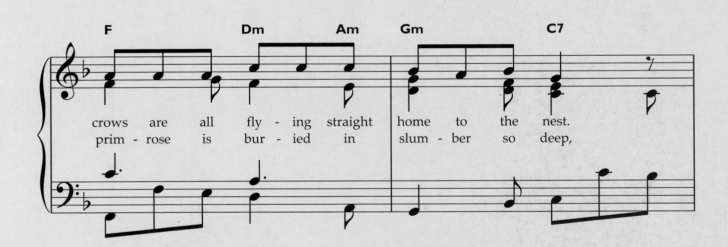

crows are all fly-ing straight home to the nest.
prim-rose is bur-ied in slum-ber so deep,

"Caw" says the crow as she flies ov-er-head, "It's
Closed for the night are the ro-ses so red, "It's

39

time   lit – tle   peo – ple   were   go – ing   to   bed!"
time   lit – tle   peo – ple   were   go – ing   to   bed!"

The butterfly drowsy has folded its wing,
The bees are returning, no more the birds sing.
Their labour is over, their nestlings are fed,
It's time little people were going to bed.

Goodnight, little people, goodnight and goodnight,
Sweet dreams to your eyelids till dawning of light,
The evening has come, there's no more to be said,
It's time little people were going to bed.

I'll put you, myself, my baby, to slumber,
Not as 'tis done by the clownish number,
A yellow blanket and coarse sheet bringing,
But in golden cradle that's softly swinging

To and fro, lu la lo,
To and fro, my bonnie baby!
To and fro, lu la lo,
To and fro, my own sweet baby!

I'll put you, myself, my baby, to slumber,
On sunniest day of the pleasant summer,
Your golden cradle on smooth lawn laying,
'Neath murmuring boughs that the birds are swaying

To and fro, lu la lo,
To and fro, my bonnie baby!
To and fro, lu la lo,
To and fro, my own sweet baby!

Irish Lullaby

Slumber, my babe! may the sweet sleep woo you,
And from your slumbers may health come to you
May all diseases now flee and fear you,
May sickness and sorrow never come near you!

To and fro, lu la lo,
To and fro, my bonnie baby!
To and fro, lu la lo,
To and fro, my own sweet baby!

Slumber, my babe! may the sweet sleep woo you,
And from your slumbers may health come to you,
May bright dreams come, and come no other,
And I be never a sonless mother!

To and fro, lu la lo,
To and fro, my bonnie baby!
To and fro, lu la lo,
To and fro, my own sweet baby!

Rock The Cradle

Traditional

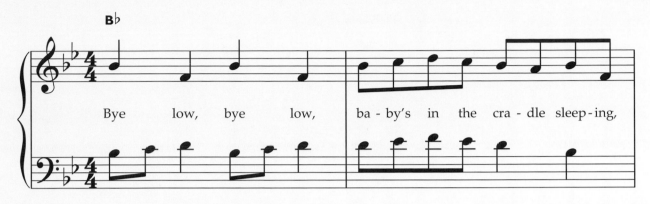

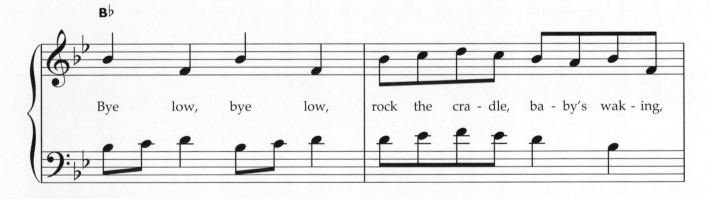

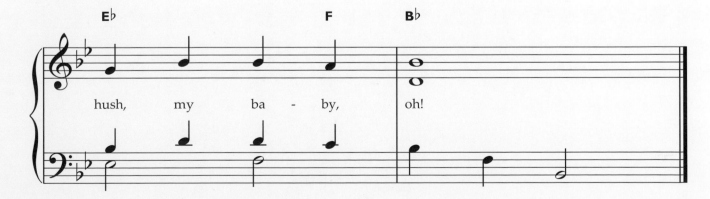

43

Sleep On, Little One

Composed by Johannes Brahms

45

dream____ the   night____ a -   way.

The____ bud - ding   trees wave   to   and fro,   And____

46

mur - mur   soft   and   low.

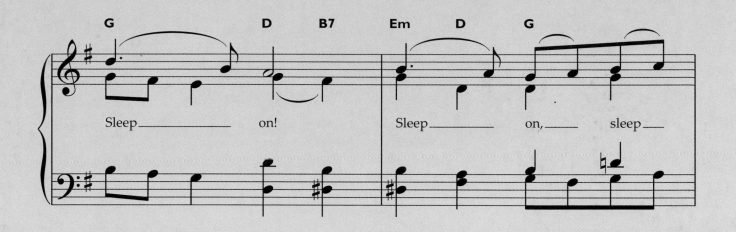

Sleep_____ on! Sleep_____ on,_____ sleep_____

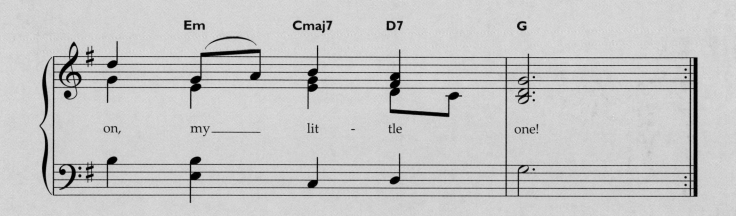

on, my_____ lit - tle one!

Day And Night

Traditional

By day the sha - dows slip a - way, At

even - ing back they creep._____ The

sun gives light___ e - nough for play, The

49

stars___ e - nough for sleep._____

O Hush Thee, My Baby

Traditional

51

All The World Is Sleeping

Traditional

Go   to   sleep   up - on   my   breast,____

All   the   world   is   sleep - ing.

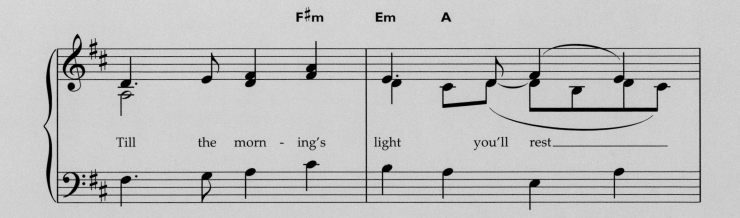

Till   the   morn - ing's   light   you'll   rest____

53

Mo - ther watch is keep - - ing.

Birds and beasts have closed their eyes,___

54

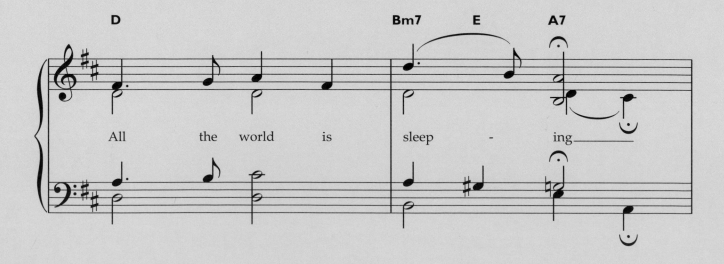

All the world is sleep - ing___

In the morn the sun will rise,——

Mo - ther watch is keep - ing.

Sweet Be Your Sleep

Traditional

57

Far In The Wood

Anonymous

Far in the wood__ you'll find a well, with

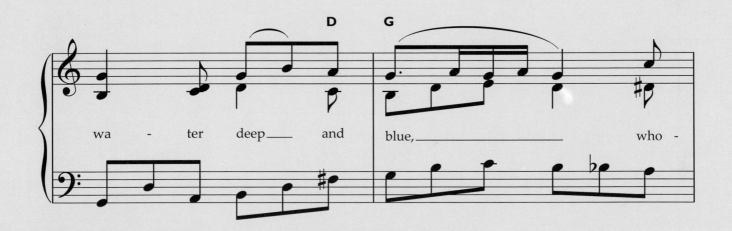

wa - ter deep__ and blue,_____ who -

ev - er drinks by moon - light clear, ti -

59

-ri,   ti - ra,   ti - ra - la - la - la,   will

live_____ a thou - sand years,_____ will

live_____ a thou - sand years._____

And all around the little well are seven lovely trees,

They rock and sway and sing a song,

Ti-ri, ti-ra, ti-ra-la-la-la,

And whisper in the breeze, and whisper in the breeze.

And through the seven lovely trees the evening wind will blow,

And down fall seven little dreams,

Ti-ri, ti-ra, ti-ra-la-la-la.

My baby all for you, my baby all for you.

Sleep! Sleep! Beauty bright,
Dreaming o'er the joys of night;
Sleep! Sleep! In thy sleep
Little sorrows sit and weep.

Sweet babe, in thy face
Soft desires I can trace,
Secret joys and secret smiles,
Little pretty infant wiles.

A Cradle Song
William Blake

As thy softest limbs I feel,
Smiles as of the morning steal
O'er thy cheek, and o'er thy breast
Where thy little heart does rest.

O! The cunning wiles that creep
In thy little heart asleep.
When they little heart does wake
Then the dreadful lightnings break,

From thy cheek and from thy eye,
O'er the youthful harvests nigh.
Infant wiles and infant smiles
Heaven and Earth of peace beguiles.

Rumanian Lullaby

Sleep, my baby, sleep and hour,
You're my little gillyflower!
Mother rocks you; mother's near!
She will wash you, baby dear.
Wash you clean in water clear,
Keep the sunshine from you here!
Sleep, my baby, sleep an hour,
Grow up like the gillyflower!

Little Bo-Peep

Traditional

63

Then up she took her little crook,
Determined for to find them.
She found them indeed, but it made her heart bleed,
For they'd left their tails behind them.

Kerry Lullaby

Traditional

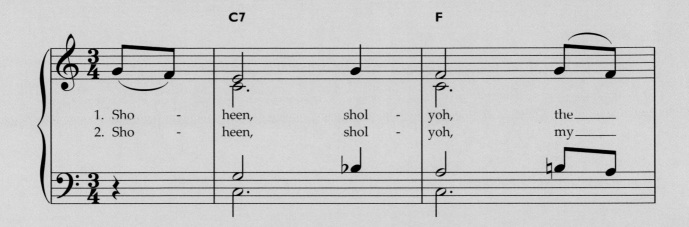

65

Hush
Lu   O,   my

trea - sure   is   dream   -   ing,   Lu,
miles   now   are   beam   -   ing   Sho -

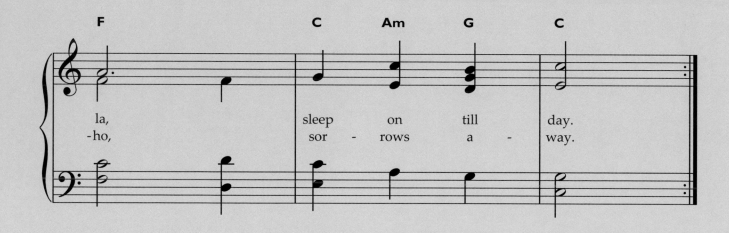

la,   sleep   on   till   day.
-ho,   sor   -   rows   a   -   way.

Sho   -   heen,   shol - yoh,   in your

white cra - dle ly - ing, God___ give you

m'lean - abh, your night's sweet re - pose.

Coventry Carol

Traditional

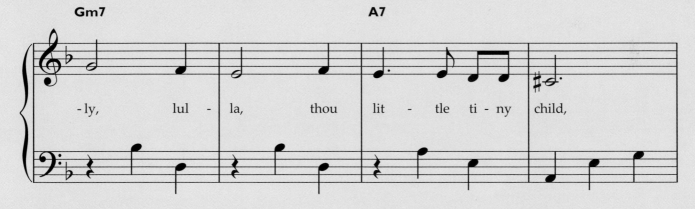

69

Coventry Carol

Hush-A-Bye, Baby

Traditional

Hush - a-bye, Ba - by,

on the tree top, When the wind blows the cra - dle will rock.

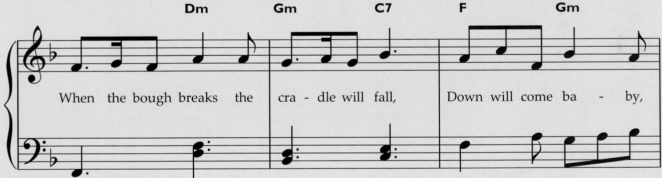

When the bough breaks the cra - dle will fall, Down will come ba - by,

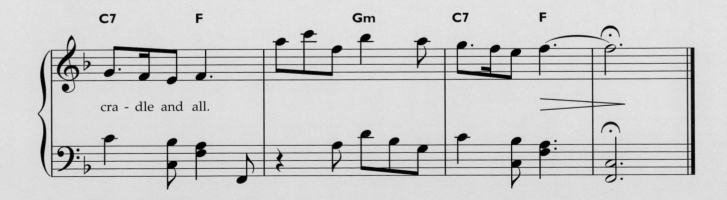

cra - dle and all.

71

Little Children

Composed by Wolfgang Amadeus Mozart

1. Lit - tle child - ren ti - ny child - ren, So
2. In their bed with down - y pil - lows, So The

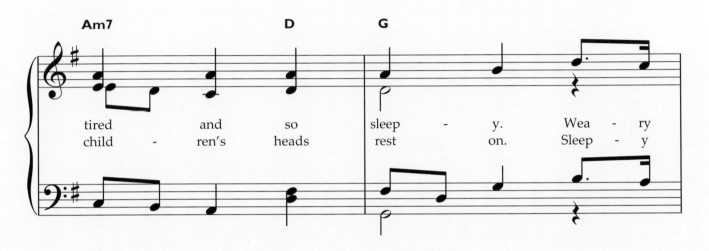

tired and so sleep - y. Wea - ry
child - ren's so heads rest on. Sleep - y

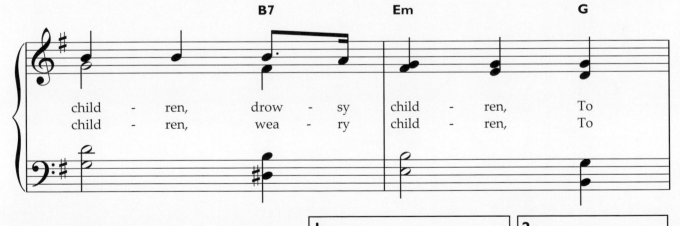

child - ren, drow - sy child - ren, To
child - ren, wea - ry child - ren, To

dream - land will go.
dream - land will have gone.

73

Mocking Bird

Traditional

Hush, lit - tle ba - by, don't say a word,

Pa - pa's gon - na buy you a mock - ing bird.

If that mock - ing bird don't sing.

75

And if that diamond ring turns brass,
Papa's gonna buy you a looking glass,
And if that looking glass gets broke,
Papa's gonna buy you a Billy goat.

And if that Billy goat don't pull,
Papa's gonna buy you a cart and bull,
And if that cart and bull turn over,
Papa's gonna buy you a dog named Rover.

And if that dog named Rover don't bark,
Papa's gonna buy you a horse and cart,
And if that horse and cart fall down,
You'll still be the sweetest little baby in town.

As soon as the fire burns red and low
And the house upstairs is still,
She sings me a queer little sleepy song
Of sheep that go over the hill.

The good little sheep run quick and soft;
Their colours are grey and white;
They follow their leader, nose and tail,
For they must be home by night.

The Sleepy Song

And one slips over, and one comes next,
And one runs after behind;
The grey one's nose at the white one's tail,
The top of the hill they find.

And when they get to the top of the hill,
They quietly slip away;
But one runs over and one comes next
Their colours are white and grey.

And one slips over and one comes next,
The good little, grey little sheep!
I watch how the fire burns red and low,
And she says that I all asleep.

Wee Willie Winkie

Traditional

Wee Wil - lie Win - kie runs through the town,

up - stairs and down - stairs in his night - gown.

Rap - ping at the win - dow, cry - ing through the lock,

are the child - ren all in bed, for now it's eight o' - clock.

79

Twinkle, Twinkle, Little Star

Traditional

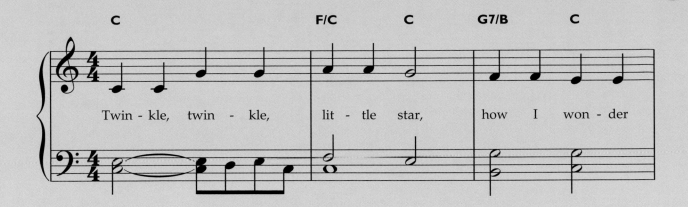

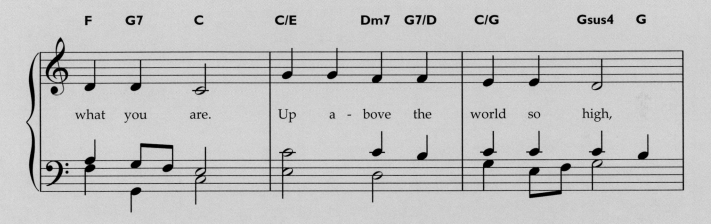

81

Gaelic Cradle Song

Traditional

83

Hush the rain sweeps o'er the knowes,* Sister goes to seek the cows,

Where they roam, where they roam, But baby sleeps at home, at home.

*ewes

Manx Lullaby

Traditional

O_____ hush thee, my dove, O

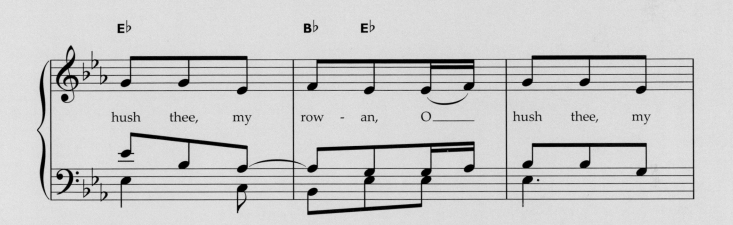

hush thee, my row - an, O_____ hush thee, my

lap - wing, my lit - tle brown bird.

Fine

85

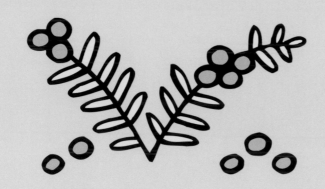

O___ fold thy___ wing and___ seek thy___

nest now, O___ shine the___ ber - ry___

86

on the bright tree, The___ bird is___

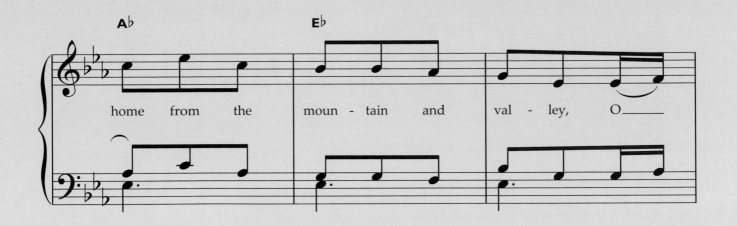

home from the mountain and valley, O

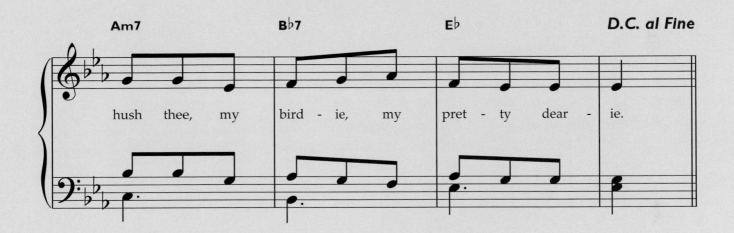

hush thee, my bird-ie, my pret-ty dear-ie.

D.C. al Fine

Now The Day Is Over

Composed by Joseph Barnaby

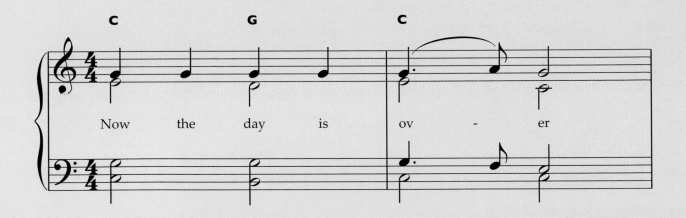

Now the day is ov - er

night is draw-ing___ nigh,_____ Sha - dows of the

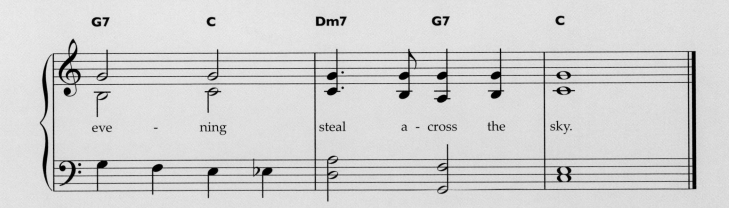

eve - ning steal a - cross the sky.

89

Lavender's Blue

Traditional

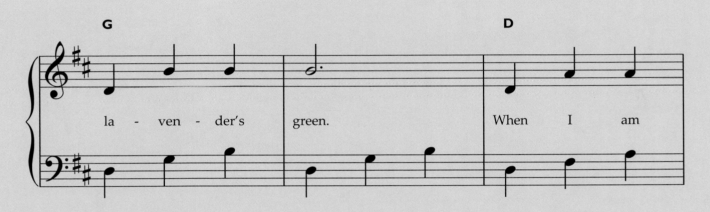

Who told you so, dilly dilly,
Who told you so?
'Twas my own heart, dilly dilly,
That told me so.

Call up your friends, dilly dilly,
Set them to work.
Some to the plough, dilly dilly,
Some to the fork.

Some to the hay, dilly dilly,
Some to thresh corn.
Whilst you and I, dilly dilly,
Keep ourselves warm.

Lavender's Blue, dilly dilly,
Lavender's green.
When you are King, dilly dilly,
I shall be Queen.

Who told you so, dilly dilly,
Who told you so?
'Twas my own heart, dilly dilly,
That told me so.

91

Sleep, Baby, Sleep

Traditional

Sleep, ba - by, sleep._____ Your

dad - dy's tend - ing the sheep._____ Your

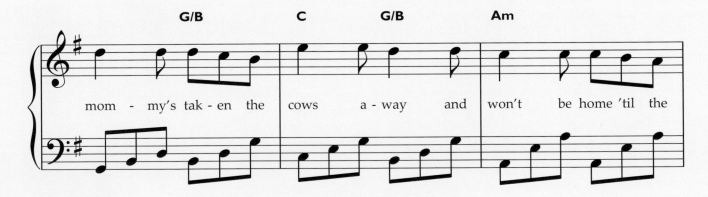

mom - my's tak - en the cows a - way and won't be home 'til the

break of day. Sleep, ba - by sleep.

93

Sleep, baby, sleep,
Our cottage vale is deep,
The little lamb is on the green,
With snowy fleece so soft and clean,
Sleep, baby, sleep.

Nature's Goodnight

Traditional

1. Clouds of gray are in the sky,
2. Bree - zes bring a breath of snow,

Flocks of birds are wing - ing by,
To their homes are the squir - rels go,

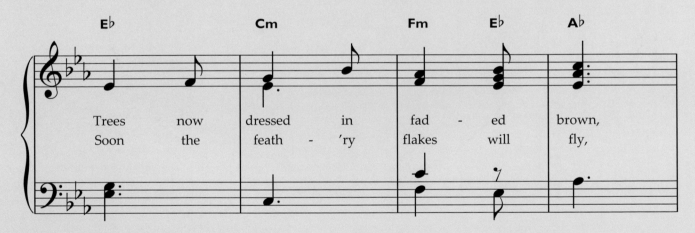

Trees now dressed in fad - ed brown,
Soon the feath - 'ry flakes will fly,

Send their leaves all rust - ling down.
Drift - ing from a win - try sky.

95